ORIGIN STORIES

by April Tierney

Copyright © 2020 April Tierney
Cover Art Copyright © 2020 Lisa Cheney-Philp

FIRE FEEDERS PRESS
Colorado

All rights reserved.

ISBN: 9798669742652

For the future ones.

CONTENTS

Part 1

Wild Onions	2
Reclamation	3
Origin Stories	5
The Honey of Words	8
Scarred-skin Nation	10
Rituals to Live By	12
The Loom of Time	14

Part 2

Sometimes Snow	18
The Direction of Home	20
Beauty-making	22
Consequence	23
Of the Mountain	26

Part 3

Rural U.S. of A.	28
Beauty in the Barren	31
Something of Love	32
Awakening	34
Our Burdens	35
Silk Cloth	37

Hiking at Thirty-two	39

Part 4

Another Story	42
Undone	44
To My Love on Your Birthday	45
Your Worktable	47
Grendel's Cousin	49
Kindred Flesh and Bone	50
Ravished	51

Part 5

Applewood	54
Daybreak	56
Sacrifices Made	57
Truthful Impressions	59
Urban Daze	60
The Greatest Love Affair	61

Part 6

Sauntering	64
Earthen Howl	66
Refuge	69
Resurrection	71
Stay	72
Unbidden	73

Part 7

Fistfuls of Light	76
Rising Dreams	78
Dear Wayward Writer	79
Reciprocity	81
Face Contortions	82
The Truth of Nature	85
The Love I Know	87

Part 8

Provenance	90
Elusivity	91
Diminished	92
Revelation	94
Rendering	96
In the Very End	97
The Company We Keep	98
Acknowledgements	101
About the Author	103

Part 1: Survive *v.* from Latin *supervivere* live beyond, live longer than (*super-* over, beyond + *vivere* to live).

WILD ONIONS

All summer long I wander the woods
collecting wild onions. They grow humbly
beneath juniper bush and pine tree,
standing neighborly beside granite and grass.

I carry them home in a bouquet,
admiring their sweet fragrance
and impossibly delicate blossoms.
When I eat their smooth, white bulbs

I taste the forest. And I miss them
when summer gives way to autumn,
then wraps itself up and inside
of winter, slowly blowing kisses

to spring. Only then,
in the earliest nights of May
do I begin to dream of them—
their slender bodies stirring
beneath the thawing soil,

their nodding heads pushing upward
to be warmed again by that handsome
lover of life. And I realize
they are sprouting in me too,
all green and delicious

all delighted by the dew
and croaking frogs, thrusting
their long cry into the
listening heart of creation.

RECLAMATION

In the beginning
there was only beauty—

what have we done with it?
Have we held it in our hands,
singing praise to the tiny
flowering faces of spring
and their flagrant generosity?
Have we reached deep
into our pockets

to offer more than we have
as a way of reclamation,
not for what we've lost
but for our own sense
of lostness?

Have we followed the tracks
laid out before us
always

winding their way around what
is devastatingly mysterious?

Have we listened
beyond the edges

of our own imagination

to the world's longing,
shot straight through us?

To the sharp flap of the bird's wings
overhead and the blinding brightness
of the morning sun's voice

until we overhear
the inception of this story
pushing through the fervent dirt

and know it is not about us,

nor was it ever intended
for such impoverished
gestures passed down
through the generations.

ORIGIN STORIES

My family, we are faithful feeders of raspberries.
My mom, uncle, grandpa, great aunt, great grandparents,
and likely further back still; only those stories were left
in the fields of Russia, and before that Germany,
where our people courted their love of labor
for the land that sustained them.

Each place I moved, and if there was even a tiny patch of soil,
my mom would transplant a few of her raspberry bushes
into my new home. Come spring she'd dig up the young roots
from her own garden, wrap them with damp newspaper
and make the hour commute to deliver these red beauties
to my front door. (While I was never in the car
during such occasions, I know she spoke to them
the entire time—soothing their fears, telling stories
of their new home). When she arrived, I'd watch her slender
hands cradle each package with the utmost care and even a hint
of pride. My mom knew she held the seeds to our family
there in her arms. She was quiet and concentrated
as she gently laid them into the Earth
which she prayed would now feed her daughter
for a very long time. "Speak to them often," she'd say,
once the soil had been laid. "They will need water daily
until their roots take. After that, every other day unless
it is very hot. Feed them coffee grounds, egg shells,
and your praise." I took mental notes, as I would years later
each time the nurses gave instructions on how to tend
to my mom after taking her home from the hospital.
She referred to the raspberries as our ancestors. And they are.

One day after one of my mom's many blood transfusions,
I asked her to show me my great grandparents old home,
so I could visualize the place where our family's raspberries
first set their feet. We had lunch nearby, then drove
to a worn down house with broken shutters
on the corner of a very busy street,

just behind a convenience store with a neon sign.
"This all used to be farmland," she assured me,
but I could not imagine it. We parked the car and walked
up to the front door, knocked, then waited awkwardly.
When no one answered, we went around to the side
and peered over the rickety fence. There was not a single
raspberry bush to be seen; instead, a big, dry plot of dirt.
"The patch used to take up this entire yard," she said,
and then I began to see them once gleaming there
in the afternoon light. "My grandparents had a farm stand
in front of the house," she went on, "where they would sell
on Saturdays. They had me come over to help pick, but mostly
I huddled under the tall leaves and ate. There were so many
that my grandma used to freeze, can, and make preserves,
but the syrup she used was too sweet. I liked them best fresh."

A few years earlier, my mom's hair started falling out
from all the chemo. So we went to a wig shop
and found something she felt comfortable in
then invited her hairdresser over to the house.
She sat in a chair in the kitchen as a razor sent fine silver
strands down to the cool tile floor (the very hair she hated
all of her life because it was not curly, but straight).
When the shaving was complete I gathered up the pieces, with
the same care as I watched her hands carry the raspberry roots
into my home so many years before. We went outside to kneel
beside her bushes, already so tall and healthy in the mid-
summer heat. We offered her hair to the soil, praying
it would feed the raspberries well so they might feed my mom
in return and help restore her strength. We cried and held
one another there in the yard while the world continued around
us—a neighbor mowing the lawn, kids playing chase.

And they did feed her well for the next few years. At the peak
of each season she would gather a bowlful of bright rubies
every other day (delight splattered all over her face)
while I would savor a very modest handful from my own
backyard. I obviously needed to speak to them more.

Then, in the final summer of my mom's life, the raspberries
ripened at least a month early, so they could continue feeding
her right up to the very end. The day before she died,
and not too long after food had lost its charm, I went out
into her garden to pick the ones who were red and willing.
I carried them into her room in a small heart-shaped dish
and put them on the bed beside her. She picked up
our ancestors one at a time and smiled as she put them
into her tired mouth, savoring their sweetness.
Of course, she offered me half

and we had our last meal together.

THE HONEY OF WORDS

In the poetry section of my favorite used book store,
I stumble across a living treasure (as I usually do)
and hurry to the cashier to pay before anyone else
has a chance to covet what I have discovered.

But who am I kidding? No one wants this book,
no one really reads books anymore.

For six dollars and fifty cents,
I take home two hundred and seventy
pages of poetry (do you know how rare it is
for that much verse from the same author
to stand bound by a single spine?).

Eating the Honey of Words
by Robert Bly, with his buxom signature
scrawled in blue ink on the third page,

proceeding a succession of crisp,
un-fingered pages all the way to
the very end. It appears as though

no one has ever read this book before,
nor certainly loved it in the way the
brilliant poet poured so much of
his life and now wintering mind.

An astounding amount of work,
devotion, deep and unarguable listening,
reduced to the amount of change
I have bumbling around in my tiny purse.

So I spend an entire
summer afternoon
extravagantly eating
the honey of Bly's words—

I underline his rolling wisdom
with my blue pen, folding the pages
this way and that, so they might know their necessity
amidst the screen-faced Gods of this computerized world.

So I might return to their fleshy magic on occasion
when I forget where I am going, or from whence I came.

SCARRED-SKIN NATION

Come now

tell us
what you
long for

and how different it is
from the country
in which you live.

How the teeth of this place
might be tempered

by your willingness to feed
what lies beneath our exiled feet.
And how the future ones are beckoned
by all the time you give to learning

the stories of the suppressed voices that
use to ring here; how they too longed after
the decency of a well-tended life. Then
your capacity to recall the song-lines
of your hard-won kin, and all they had

to starve, flee, or fight
so that you could finally settle
into the arms of a reasonably
comfortable home, even on the
most cold and despairing of nights.

So that you could gather
with other heart-ravaged
humans to dream into
where it all went wrong

and what is now needed

for things to be made right.

How the firm lines
of separation
might be blurred
into alchemical
circles of healing;

how we hand-spin, sew, and
weave colorful prayer flags
to wave across the wild wind,

planted with permission
into the softened soil
of a scarred-skin nation
in which we live.

RITUALS TO LIVE BY

One winter day I went out for a walk
as the temperature composed poetry

to that cold heart which is
the single digits of February.
The air made swift and sharp
scalpel cuts through my jeans,
carving both legs into icicles
while my lungs receded into
useless sacks of stone. Even still
I headed for Wonderland Lake,

purely for the purpose of claiming
some modest fragment of sanity
amidst the insanity swelling
around the margins of our days.

I only made it to the lip of that basin
and not a step further, before fully freezing
in place. There was a clump of downy ducks
huddled together, atop a thick coat of ice;
I stood and watched as the cold smashed
shards of frost all over my stupefied face.

I will tell you now,
this is what happened
(and I promise it is true):

All the ducks abruptly stood, then
gingerly rearranged themselves—
there was one that was being warmed
in the middle of their fine circle
who graciously moved to the rim,
while some outlying fellow
found his way into the center—
then they all sat again

as cleanly as they had stood.

Several minutes passed and
the ritual repeated itself. They
all got up, the one in the middle
kindly waddled to the outer ring
while another brown and bopping
bird stepped into the center. And
once again, they hunkered down.

There was no arguing
about who would go next
and no one appeared to be
keeping close track of time.

Their fat wrapped bodies knew
when to move, who needed warming,
and how long it would take to patiently,
rhythmically keep that little raft alive.

It was a wondrous thing to behold.
So innate, considerate, resourceful.
They warmed one another as I stood
on the shore, watching and shivering

alone. I stayed for one more round
of this unchoreographed propriety,
then turned back around and headed
for the house—eyeballs numb, heart
throbbing with fortified and feathery

love. So this is how it happens, I thought.
This is how we usher one another
through the most impossible
width of our days.

THE LOOM OF TIME

I don't know anymore what this life is for
but sorrow and astonishment.

How can we sincerely feed
our needful place

until we've sat and prayed
on the lonesome steps
at death's door?

Our hands and voices trembling
with all that we could ever afford.

How can we stoke the fires
of the village hearth,
until we know what it is
to be betrayed by blood?
Until we've tasted that metal
draining down our silenced throats
and thirst for something more.

How can we saddle up to the loom of time,
weaving stories and the continuation
of beauty's true name, until we've learned
what it means to properly fail and age?

Planting our kisses onto the cheeks of all
that we love and may never seen again.

How can we understand
what it means to give
our well-longed-for gifts
to the world, until we've cried
out into the center of a
star-spattered night?

And how can we say our final goodbyes
until we've gazed into the darkened eyes
of every day's lawful ending?

Finally seeing that
these are the moments
for which we were made.

Part 2: Earwigs are the only insects who mother their young.

SOMETIMES SNOW

Stay close my child.
Remember why
you are here.

~

The wind may writhe hard
into the crevasse of night,
cracking trees to their core,

and the fiddle strings
might snap sharp
across the limits
of your veneration.

~

Sometimes snow
arrives so late
all the blossoms
on their lofty branches
die at the dawn
of their intoxication.

Yet, your fingers still freeze
as you walk the streets
of winter,

trying in earnest to record
everything into the pale body
of your tiny notebook.

But do not place all of your faith
on the page alone. It can not
bear such blundering weight.

~

Stay open my child—

the way you live
is the means by which
you will remember.

THE DIRECTION OF HOME

I once met a Kurdish woman, her face
a constellation of memories, her eyes
two stars gleaming in an otherwise
starless night. She'd been living
in North America for twenty-two years,

but for the whole twenty minutes of our
unbroken conversation, her body
faced in the direction of the home
she once fled. "Land is like your mother,"
she told me. "It shapes and sustains you.

I left half
of my body
over there.
I will never
get it back."

As she spoke, her wide hand found its way
to the silver railing of a staircase where
we stood, awkwardly. She clutched on, as if
afraid of otherwise toppling over. When I inquired

about her family, she said, "My father still lives there.
He is eighty-two. My husband and I watch the news
every single day to see how our family is doing.
There is so much oppression, poverty, and murder.
This endless war for oil and greed..." Her voice
trailed off, then momentarily re-caught its
thread. "My heart breaks continuously,"
she said, with no apparent need

for consolation. Her dark eyes
studied mine, wanting to know
if I could fathom the things
she had felt and seen.

I shook my head. No,
I could not. And yet, I still

believed her, even if
my limited imagination
could not find a home
for her perfect shape of grief.

"My doctor tells my husband and I
that we must stop watching the news,"
she admitted. "Our blood pressure is too high,
our depression is too great. But we cannot.
When you love a place, it is impossible to turn away."

She paused then and sighed. Looking around
where we stood—children running past
laughing, and the bright mountain sun
slapping color across our naked shoulders
and cheeks. "Of course, I'm thankful," she nodded,
"to have raised my son and daughter here, in a place
that is safe and where they have everything
that they could possibly want.

But sometimes, having everything is not enough."
Then she continued up the staircase and into the day.

BEAUTY-MAKING

A thousand years before we were born,
it was the artists' exquisite choice of color
and candor which made the world spill forth.

And a thousand years after we die,
it will be those same brave souls
who will revive the lifeblood
of our culture, refusing
to buy into the belief that their

crafts and carefully calloused hands
are no longer a human-scaled necessity.

How could they fall for the tale
of one God creating everything,
when they know how intimately
many Gods and Goddesses
work through their willing bodies

to pour liquid beauty
into the opened mouths
of a parched planet?

And what of you,
curator of magic?

Warming milk with honey
late at night to help lull your child
into the dreaming. Or the many stories
that your parted lips make pilgrimages to,
and how the walls of the house
bend their heads in to listen.

CONSEQUENCE

One Wednesday morning in the middle of July,
my friend's sister visited the Royal Gorge Bridge
in Cañon City, walked to the middle and jumped

nine hundred and fifty-five feet
to the rapids below; the same rapids where
I have whitewater rafted—screaming and laughing
beside five other people, with paddles plunging
directly into the heart of that Arkansas River—
three years, or three lifetimes ago. It is now Saturday night
and I have just received the news of this woman's death.

A woman whom I have never met, yet I am plagued
with the image of her body sailing through the air
above the place where my body once swam,
padded by a yellow life-vest and plastic helmet.

The rapids were fierce that day and they tossed us all
around our patched-up raft. But, there was a single stretch
of water that opened her arms to us, where we paused
to catch our breath and thank the River Goddess
for looking kindly on our insensible afternoon of play.
No one else wanted to jump in, the water was too crisp
but I could not resist. Our guide and friend instructed me
to keep my feet up, so I laid my head back and floated,
gazing toward that metal bridge strung so high
between the red walls of the canyon.

I know nothing of this woman
other than that both of our mothers died
within a few months of each other,
which somehow makes us kin.

Was there not proper support for her grief
in all this time afterward? Or all those years before,
when her mom was kept alive on tubes?

Surely she must have brushed cheeks with insanity then,
when the medical industry continued to torture
her mother's body in the name of some
Hippocratic oath. Or perhaps it was hypocrisy,

whose roots reach back to Old French
ypocresie, meaning false appearance of virtue.
And now we're inching closer to the truth.

This surely was how I first lost my mind—
when the doctors told my mom that her cancer
had progressed to stage four, meaning she would die

but no one mentioned this, they only proceeded
to prescribe more rounds of chemo, radiation,
blood thinners, CT scans and MRIs, steroids,
immunotherapy, anti-nausea, pain and sleep meds,
blood transfusions, regular check-ups to monitor
weight, appetite, blood pressure, and depression.

Yet, when I questioned the sanctity and sanity
of continuing to "treat" somebody who was already dying,
they made it seem as though I was the one who was insane.
I called my mom's doctor after the cancer had spread
to her skin, breast, brain, and spine to plead with him—
based on his many years of experience and the thousands
of patients he witnessed wither away—to tell me
in all approximation, how much longer she had left.

Do you know what he said to me, as I knelt
on the living room floor weeping? "I am uncomfortable
having this conversation with you. It is entirely inappropriate
as no one can say how long your mom will live but God."

There was no compassion offered to me there, strung out
into those ghostly waters where I was nearly drowning.
The prominent cancer doctor was downright offended
that someone would even speak of death in his direction.

So when, I wondered, was it appropriate to utter death's name,
when it had clearly been feasting from our table for so long?
Each day, I watched my mom's body turn more fully toward
that opened door while everyone else was pretending
a miracle would occur. But, when you've tortured
a person past the point of recognition,

perhaps death is that very miracle.
And then there is my friend's sister's body
mangled among the foaming waves
and jagged rocks.

Now, do not tell me there is no consequence
for a dishonored death. It is written on the scarred skin
of all the world's daughters. Those ones who bear the wombs
of the women who birthed them, the ones
who were forbidden to die when it was their time.
We're told to busy ourselves with worrying
about whether what we might say
will make someone else feel uncomfortable.
So we choke on our silences. But some daughters
cannot stand the pain, horror, and extreme isolation

of memories seared into their purple veins.
And so with all that I've seen and still
remember of the wretched manipulation,
irreverence, and disorientation,

I think of my friend's sister
and I am astonished
I am still here.

OF THE MOUNTAIN

"Imagine being a mountain," he said
in passing, as if this were something
worthy of the most brief consideration.

I have sat at the feet of many magnificent mountains;
walked up their spines, praised their wildflowers,
and made offerings to their tributaries, streaming
like silver strands down their steep cheeks and
rugged backs. I even shouted my wedding vows,
swathed inside their wild arms. But to be one?
Admittedly, I've not considered it before.

Maybe it's because I was born in their midst; their blue
and purple silhouettes standing guard over my crib,
with their long, green fingers swaying and strumming me
deeper into the world's dreaming. Over the years,
their chiseled rocks shaping my body in response
to all this wandering and wondering. So then

I must be *of* the mountain,
which is why I've not inquired
about becoming one before.

Part 3: Grieve *v.* from Latin *gravare* make heavy or burdensome, from *gravis* weighty, grave.

RURAL U.S. OF A.

It is Sunday, and I
along with the whole wide world
here at the anklebone of the Rocky Mountains,
have listened to the onslaught of gunshots

cresting in disquieting waves like a war on replay,
over and over again for most of the day. Finally
I thought, this cannot be legal, and phoned my neighbor

who has lived here longer than I have
and loves this land in ways that I
am only beginning to fathom.

She had never heard anything like this before
and confessed her kids were very upset.
Which was enough to persuade me
to call the county sheriff,

who confirmed it is entirely legal
to shoot guns as often as one pleases
on your own property; that this is why
country folk move so far away from HOAs
and the expanding hordes of people.

But what about the greening hillsides, I wondered?
Or the caterpillars wrestling toward flight
in their fragile cocoons? Does anyone care
that the bumble bee has important work to do,
that this endless disturbance might permanently
alter his mood? "Isn't there a noise ordinance?"
I asked. "Only at night," he cooly replied,

as if no living thing should require refuge
during the day. "But it sounds dangerous,"
I insisted. "Like someone is drunk and rampant.
I understand target practice, my husband is a hunter;

but who needs so many bullets? It's around ten to
fifteen shots every five to ten minutes, and this
has been going on for several hours."

"Rampant shooting is also legal," he replied.
"Just as long as they are not wrongfully hunting
or directing their aim toward anyone else's property."
Then he laughed, "I actually would love to move
out your way so I could also exercise my right
to shoot my gun as often as I would like."

There was nothing left to discuss,
so we said our flat goodbyes
and then I looked up the etymology
of the word rampant.

adj. Before 1382 *raumpaunt* fierce, ravenous;
earlier, rearing or standing on hind legs (about 1300);
borrowed from Old French *rampant*.

I understand this. Sometimes I rear on hind legs, too;
when a person has disgraced someone I love, or
when a hailstorm threatens to trample my young seedlings
in spring. I roar in these moments, I am fierce
in my willingness to favor the continuation of life.

But these are fleeting moments.
To entertain them for long periods
seems unreasonable, unnecessary.
Far more reckless than useful.

And so, a good while after the rampage finally stops,
I watch the trees lean their backs into the stillness
and the wildflowers lift their faces in relief.

The birds come cautiously to sing their tiny songs
into the shell-shocked air. I wonder where they went
during those long hours of hiding, if the elk and deer

will ever trust our human hands again?

"This is something you might as well get used to,"
the officer said blithely over an unhurried
and unconcerned call. No, I decide,
this kind of absurdity will never
masquerade as normal for me.

BEAUTY IN THE BARREN

There is desecration
all around us.

But there is also
beauty

standing tall and proud
in the barren fields—

their tiny arms
and voices

twisting toward
the rising sun.

Let us get down
on our knees—

let us learn to bend
our heads again

in the direction of
those prayerful stories

pointing
the way home.

SOMETHING OF LOVE

One day

you'll watch your brother
looking through old photos
of your dead mother

the corners of his lips
curved skyward
like a crescent moon
laying on her back,
with feet and arms
stretched toward
something strange,

yet familial.
Every now
and again
he'll pause

to carefully lift a single
glistening image
up and into the day.

He'll murmur memories
far out across the summer
landscape and you'll listen,

longing to remember,
too. He'll take his time,
sighing and struggling to
to recall the words,
which accompany
the stories

that speak kindly
to the face

beaming back at him
through that four-by-six frame.

On this day,
you will learn
something of love;

you will discover the sound
it makes when rambling through
the hillsides of gravestones and grace.

AWAKENING

I see you everywhere
and in everything.
Is this the world
you've dreamt
into being?

Am I living
into its
awakening?

Please, do not lay bare
the answers now,
for I am not yet faithful
enough to shelter them.

Let me be in awe
a few lifetimes more;
let me prove myself

trustworthy
of your inquiry.

OUR BURDENS

How straightforward
each day would be
if we never had to
stare down the torments
of society. If the wall
we've built up and around
our tenderized hearts
was in fact a physical thing

with concrete, steel bars,
and other refineries—

all to prevent our bodies
from being swayed
by the sob or confusion
of life having its sweet way
with our inseparable souls.

There are so many people
who never speak of the things
they feel or see; who never

stand in the middle
of their private lives
to howl or weep.
How does one keep
so composed

during such cantankerous times?
And why would you want to?
When I am so often crippled
by despair, I pray for the tiniest
bit of courage to reach out
my hand and call you in close

to confront the lie

which lays waste
to our burdens—

the one that claims
everything
is supposed to be
swallowed in secret—

shoving all the world
right out of our lives.

SILK CLOTH

I have a friend
whose grandmother
stopped speaking
the last two years of her life.
They cut a hole into her throat
and removed her voice box,

leaving the dark cavern open like a crater
in the middle of her slender neck,
which she covered with a silk cloth.

My friend learned to read her grandmother's eyes,
hearing the words she hid beneath the silence,
long after everyone else stopped paying attention.
This was their secret vein of communication.

Recently, my friend needed a place to stay
so, she slept in the spare bedroom in our basement.
She cried a lot, but otherwise ate very little
and was as quiet as a mouse. She watched
me make food and wash the dishes,
asking if I always devoted so much
energy to such tedious things.

"I love cooking and eating," I exclaim.
"So cleaning the kitchen is an ode
to what I know as love."

I ask if she's spoken to her mother recently.
"No," she says. "Not in a long while."

I would give up all of this eating
and cleaning to call my mom,
just to hear her say hello
into the phone. Did her o's
curl out at the end like a ribbon

or fluff up like whipped cream?

I am beginning to forget
the sound of her voice,
so it's time once again
to visit her mother

whom my mother
stopped speaking to
thirty years ago, long

before she ever intended to die.
I will listen to my grandmother's hello—
probing for a sign of my mom
reaching back through the distance—
reminding me we are so very close.

I will look into my grandmother's eyes
to hear the words strangled there,
never even given a choice.

HIKING AT THIRTY-TWO

Meandering up the trail this morning,
I pass three boys briskly walking down.
The tallest exclaims, "In ten years,
we'll look back on this day and remember
how we climbed Green Mountain at eighteen!"

The boy leading the pack cuts in,
"Oh, what a disgusting time that will be!
I'm quite satisfied with my age now."

There was such resolve within this gnarled statement
that his friends were shoved right out of the conversation—
they continued past me in silence, the boy in front
smug all over his face. So I look down at my loyal legs
winding their way up the canyon; at four and a half years
past the time that first fellow just foretold, I question
if I am carrying any of the contempt that the
second fellow could already see coming at him.

I marvel at my sturdy feet, not as agile as they once were,
but typically gracious at navigating the spaces between
the red rocks now slick from last night's rain. I relish
the cool air running her fingers through my tangled hair
and smile as the birds go on to greet the day.

No, I conclude; all that remains is praise.

Part 4: Male nursery web spiders will offer an insect wrapped in silk to female spiders before mating, so that afterward she might not devour him.

ANOTHER STORY

So you are the headless man,
standing there shocked,
unable to believe
that someone else
could know something
you yourself could not
understand. You've forgotten
how to be reverent, misplaced
its purpose with all the other
memories that refuse
to stand in a line
and straighten their backs
against the bricks that
you have not assembled;
nor do you care to learn
anything of the foundation
in which they will spend
the rest of their lives
sinking into.

So you tell the Great Mystery you are busy—
there are many other things more deserving
of your time. And its sweet lips stop visiting
your doorsill, it can only kneel there
bent at the waist in supplication,
for so many relinquished days
and years. But when you look out

from where you sit
into the belly of the land
that sustains your body,
you might find another story
that arouses your good name.

And if you dare to stare
into its tearful eyes,

you might hear
the voices of the ones
you've renounced,
claiming you
for their own again,

for their vessel
and their prayer.

Then, you will remember
how disorientation arrives
as a blessing, and that it was
always meant to be this way.

UNDONE

I will walk down this path laid out before me, I will
be obedient to the dark stretch of unknown expanse
reaching past all that I can see. This is why I stand
before you now, naked; undone by enchantment and grief.
Will you have me? If the answer is no, I will stand before you
for a hundred years still; waiting, listening, forsaking
all that I suspected to be true. Then perhaps,
you will take my hand and we will paddle out to sea.

TO MY LOVE ON YOUR BIRTHDAY

Forty years ago today, the Great Mystery
unfastened its wild hands and presented the world
with this new life. Your Old Ones leaned in close
to kiss your tiny cheeks with their courage
and whisper their human-sized stories
into the russet marrow of your bones.

Then they began dreaming your future life into existence,
the very future you are walking your way into now.

They were the ones who foresaw the young boy
yearning for connection; the young man
turning his back on pretense and addiction.

They imagined the day you would sit way up
on that mountain, lightning crashing all around;
then smiled, nodding their chins in the direction
of your enduring strength. And again

when you sat out with no food or water
as wolves circled round and an eagle
soared overhead, they sighed and laid back,

heartened to find that you would face this life
with such fierce protection. Then, in our wedding days
they watched as you trembled and stood anyway,
speaking beauty into that high mountain valley—

they sang and danced in celebration.
Today, my love, they are still singing.

When you forget the kind of man that you are
or the ennobled ones that you come from,
I will remind you. And when I fall short,
the immovable trees in our new home
will call out your good name.

The deer with their fuzzy antlers in spring
and the sun with its untrimmable light,
will all look at you in recognition
as the one who dares to merge trails

with exquisite honor
and an integrous heart.
On this day of your birth,
bless the ones who made you

and bless your generous hands
which have responded
to all their generosity

by tending
to this sweet life
in return;

the hundreds, no thousands,
of others whose hearts
you have shaped as a prayer
that they might turn outward
to serve this wondrous world
just as you have promised to do.

YOUR WORKTABLE

When you seek the technique
of something—say
weaving or witchcraft
(which are the same things)—

without also courting
the places and people
who bequeathed
such perfect magic
into our fitful world,

then the spirit of this
sought-after thing
will not take its seat
at your worktable.

Why spend all those
long hours laboring alone,
when you could do so
in good company?
When you could allow
their dusty memories
to rise up through
your bloodstream

and animate your
patterned fingertips
toward ever deeper
demonstrations
of humanity.

The best incantations
spill forth their secrets
when etiquette is not
an afterthought,

but the way in which
you apprentice
the precious things
of this world—

those artful creatures
you claim to admire
and one day become.

GRENDEL'S COUSIN

"From your mouth to God's ears,"
my grandma always used to say.

Now it's from all of our mouths
to the monster's ears, the one who
has been neglected for far too many years.

The one who wanders the streets
starved, who comes to feast
on our human comforts
and frailties.

How can we feed this Rough God
in these rough and ungodly times

when amnesia is king and
all the world's nourishment
is being hoarded for the living?

KINDRED FLESH AND BONES

This ceremony began long ago,
long before you caught
the sweet scent

of its dreaming.

Now, you slowly grasp
what is being asked of you,
what is indeed required
to awaken into such a
tender-hearted dream.

All the prayers and tears—
they have prepared you
for this procession.

Your secret wrestling and wondering
fortunately, has never been too well a kept secret.
There are others who have watched you
in this endless unknowing, for they are the keepers
of what was never intended to be known.

They are the ones who have waited
all these years for you to finally need them;
for you to feed their famished bellies,
to lay out platter after platter of beauty,
to remember every bite and breath
that you take in from this world
is of their kindred flesh and bones.

RAVISHED

Take me toward the quiet murmur,
fold me in your arms; let me be a woman
decorated by such lawless delights.

Permit me to be someone
who lies bare at your side,
awed by what it means
to surely be alive.

Part 5: Winter *n*. Old Germanic word meaning time of water.

APPLEWOOD

It's sixty degrees and dry as bones.
The news says it's the driest winter
we've seen in sixty-one years—
since 1956, the year my mother was born.

Susan K. Rusch fetched her first breaths
on April 11th at Lutheran Hospital
right next door to Crown Hill Cemetery,
where most of our family is buried.

Who could have guessed
she would cast her last breaths
sixty-one years later in the hospice
of that very same hospital,

the one where she birthed
both of her children;

just down the road from her grandparent's farm
and a few streets over from the high school
that she, her parents, and grandparents all attended—
their mascot, a pitchfork-carrying farmer. But above all,
beside the lake she walked faithful circles around,
like the lover of water she always knew herself to be;
the lake her daughter and dozens of kestrels
sailed beside on the day of her death,

August 22nd, 2017.

Someone, or a great many someones,
must have known the shape
of this story's ending,

for now the skies refuse
to release their snow.

Meanwhile, my brother tells me
that on particularly cold nights
when his body is wrapped in a
warm coat, he thinks of her body
buried deep within the Earth,
and wonders if she's cold.

DAYBREAK

As the sun slowly lifts his shining head
from bed and into a different kind of dreaming,
tiny birds fly straight for our tall, eastern-facing windows.

Is it the thrill of frosted pane death that allures them?
Or have they too gone mad for the pink and orange
fingers of morning that reach out across the sky
and pull me from sleep to meet the exuberance

of the day? In either case,
those heart-stopping thumps
haunt me. And while I've never found
a dead bird on the deck, I long to open

every
single
window

so they might feel welcomed
into the mouth of the house,

where we can be foolhardy together
for the throbbing brilliance of daybreak.

SACRIFICES MADE

Some people must speak the pain
over and over again

to keep it from being stowed away
in an abandoned place,

where no one can benefit
from its shadowy light.

Others must wander the woods,
repeating incantations aloud

to protect the tiny pockets of sanity,
which remain unscathed in this world.
A few more shall stand on stage,
daring ridicule

to revive their mythic names,
to shudder in the same boots
that were stolen from their ancestors,
and to choke on the same words
that were beaten back.

Sacrifice is made
not by going without,
but by giving more
and more

and more of yourself
to that which you
may never see.

Let your stomach drop
and your voice quake;

let the ones who have walked,

danced, kneeled, and prayed
long before you

feel your courage
caressing the broken
and beating heart
of this song-filled
landscape.

Above all, it's the little ones—
looking up through their big eyes—

bare innocence bound
to their outstretched hands,
who ask, "Is this what
you've given your life to?"

Yes my child. Yes.

TRUTHFUL IMPRESSIONS

When all is quiet
and there's the briefest
of moments to hear
yourself breathe,

do not keep these
deliberations bent in
so damn close.

Listen to the sigh
of the space
forming around
what was once
so consumed
by clamor

and greed.
See the stillness
stretched out
before you
like a lover

forever burning
to bathe in your
bewildering waters,
all while knowing

every scrap of it
will be bartered away
again before long.

URBAN DAZE

The crowds hurry about
or lull about, carrying
their insatiable hunger
too close to their chests,
like crudely-wrapped packages

ever hollow and cold.
How unskillful our lives are,
bumping into one another
while leaving wonderment
to its loneliness at the
threshold of our homes.

THE GREATEST LOVE AFFAIR

My little puppy loves snow.
He buries his long, speckled snout
into her smooth bosom, breathing in
that clean, wet scent. Then

he nuzzles his little furry body
into her cold, milky flesh—
squirming around on his back,
legs twisting this way and that.

He heaves and snorts, then gets up
and pounces; a purr hiding
beneath that big, toothy smile.

He's happiest when in her arms—
sitting at the window, gazing out
the moment we come back in,

waiting for the time they can
intertwine once again.

I have yet to see
a greater love.

Part 6: When a dolphin is injured or sick and cannot surface to breathe, she emits a distress call that signals other dolphins to lift her to the surface.

SAUNTERING

When you hold a thing in your hands,
feeling its full weight lean into your

calloused or cracking skin, how do you know
where to begin? To insert your knife or thumbnail
into its own precious flesh, exposing its private life
to the whole of the world, to a wanting that now
must end. Why do you walk or write

right up to the edges, without
introducing yourself to them first?

Would you approach a Goddess in this way?
Would you expect her vigorously pumping heart
to smile into your hardened face with its immovable
impatience for everything to always be eager
and willing? Whatever happened to sauntering?
To dipping your toes or trembling fingers into the lake
before fully jumping in. To stopping where you might run,
if only to look long enough into the heart of a thing,

until it reveals its desired shape
to you. Though you continue to look,

to listen for hours
or years longer still,

so that it might bestow
some blessing
from its interior life,

the life you were
about to break into
without even asking
permission.

Now once again, feel the weight
of the thing there in your
humbled hands, pausing

to thank this treasured one
who will give its body,
so that you might breathe
and embolden another day.

EARTHEN HOWL

Last night I was speaking
with my well-meaning friend
and mother of two young children,
in a brightly-lit restaurant
which concealed all evidence
of erosion or extinction
in this big, breaking, and
exquisitely beautiful world.

The waitresses had smiles for days;
the fresh, clean cups of water were plentiful
and the food, well-seasoned. Yet even the
blue pillows of our cozy booth seats
kept me on edge. As I confessed

my concerns for the future generations,
wondering if they too will have clean water
and warm buildings to gather in
on deep winter nights,

my cells already knew
how precious these thing were
and widely unavailable to more
than an accidental few.

My friend, with her arms padded by hope and
a prostrating fear for her own children's safety
too enormous to be entertained, responded
like something from an automated teller machine:

"There is no scientific evidence that suggests
mass human extinction will happen any time soon,
at least not within the next one hundred years."

As if this should quiet my restless mind
on sleepless nights and put an end to any

further wondering about the wisdom or
mercy of bringing more babies onto this
overpopulated and under-praised planet.

She assuredly passed the baton of worry
away from her own kids' stories,
but failed to say anything for her future
grandchildren, should she be so blessed.
Or the dozens of other species that are
already disappearing every single day.

My response was slow, like a thawing
basin in unseasonable heat, but also
sure; a folktale read from the etchings
along the inner walls of life's aching bones.

"Science fails us," I said. "But if you go outside
and press your ear down onto the breathing Earth,
if you stay there a good while and listen,
she will tell you a different story."

~

Are we brave enough to feel our pain
for what is happening now,
which is her pain, too?

To not gloss over the grief in favor of feel-good
interactions, which are fleeting anyway and take
much more than they could ever give. Only then

can we know our love for the ones who birth us,
feed us, clothe our shivering bodies, and shelter
our graying heads. The ones who are not silent,
though we have forgotten how to hear
their fierce, earthen howl.

~

Now statistics are Gods—

not the thousands of tiny tips
greening with generosity
at the ends of the
many waving arms
on that evergreen tree,

who stands nobly outside your window,
watching the festivities and glowing screens,

who guards over the house
never demanding a fee.

REFUGE

What does it mean
to be natural anymore?

To take refuge
beneath the wide arms
of the ponderosa pine

and feel her shade
licking your forehead,
like a new born babe
still wet with dew
from the womb
of your mother.

To place your steps not on
but beside the bristling cactus
with his sun and salmon colored
flowers, squealing into summer.

To lay your tired body down
where tall grasses and soft sage

stand proud,

their shoulders rolled back,
chests lifted skyward,

shouting an invocation
to the changing of the guards
and the seasons.

A place where the wild raspberries
sing the songs you have forgotten,

their tiny white fingers
flaming a promise of sweetness

into the not-too-distant days
of mid-summer's profusion,

while the turkey vulture circles round
with his orange mouth and
magnificent wingspan,

making sure you haven't
decided to stay.

RESURRECTION

We watched a man nearly die;
who or what brought him back

to life? Perhaps it was the way we stood
quietly, as though gathered into the sanctified
arms of all the world's endings—

those neglected Gods of nutriment,
who praise the ebbing rhythm
in every living thing.

The way we watched as he drooped onto the woman
beside him; eyes closed and mouth slacked open,
intercepting a scream at the doorstep of his throat.
We held our collective breath too, while sweat
dribbled down his chin and swelled into a dark,
heart-shaped ring at the center of his well-ironed shirt.

When the doctor came to take his pulse, the man's eyes
flapped open. The doctor commanded him to talk,
and to not stop. So the man mouthed, "I love you so much,"
over and over again into the prayerful air. Soundless, his words
whirled around the startled room, coiling between our troubled
bodies and landing back into the delicate hands of his wife,
who was standing behind him, rubbing the sweat
from his wrinkled brow and bending every so often
to place trembling kisses atop his gray and bobbing head.

"Practice resurrection," Wendell Berry said. And so he did.

STAY

Don't go;
stay.

Stay to become
that thing

which has always
begged for your name.
Stay to see the buds
pushing toward
laughter

in spring; the wind
carving songlines
into rock,
the rock
growing moss.

Stay my love—
let us put our hands
onto that soft carpet
of greenery,

the one that hollows
out our innocence

and ties our belonging
to the things of this world,
for which we cannot keep.

UNBIDDEN

I have a friend, who
when the goldfinches
return in spring,
she sings.

Her kind face
unfolds into a vault
of jubilation, pausing
mid-sentence, to cry out
their canticle names.

I imagine the glee of those gilded birds
in finding their returning has not gone
unnoticed; but even more so
is needed and wildly acclaimed.

So while I've yet to meet
a goldfinch here in the gulch—

when I do, I'll be sure
to unlatch my lungs
and give thanks.

Part 7: In a single orbit around the Earth, the Moon always shows the same face.

FISTFULS OF LIGHT

"Preach! Preach!" The people screamed
to their preacher, who was no longer there;

for he had packed up his things
in the middle of a muffled night
and walked right out of their lives.

That preacher did not stop walking
until he reached those good,
green Irish hills where so many
of his people lived, loved,
and are buried. There
he knelt down in the grass
and lifted his hairless head
to that brilliant face, casting
her silver-tongued lacquer
all over a blue-black sky.

In response, the moon threw
fistfuls of light onto
his folded body, and handed
him back his nobility—

their names etched
handsomely onto his

aging veins,
like the crying visitors
who were cast out from this land
in heedless exchange for another.

There, with the stars and abiding shadows
as witness, that man got claimed by a place
so particular to his people

that their memory leapt up

through his throat and for the first time
since childhood, he sang songs
unshackled by scripture.

The trees leaned in to listen just then,
even the crickets paused in consideration.

The whole world had been waiting
for this moment, now nothing would be
as we thought it would be.

RISING DREAMS

Sometimes I see the faces
of the ones who used to live here

chiseled into the rocks—
foreheads furrowed, eyes
squinting into the pain.

What must it be like
to witness what we've done
with this place? To their home,

the one that wet-nursed their babies
into the crooning night and fortified
their living language with its
sunsets and stars. Sometimes,

I feel their strong arms
waving hand-spun stories
into the abandoned hills

and often the echo
resounds as a scream.

Seldom do I hear
their blessings
in the tall grasses
and drying pine needles,
huddled beneath the
tallest trees,

but when I do,
it is a crescendo
of rising dreams.

DEAR WAYWARD WRITER

What else can we look for

but clues in the writings
of other lovers of language—
those dappled and dewy provocations
aimed at an honest encounter with life?

Their probing around
in the dark corners
of the world's flesh
for a momentary
flash of light—

one that we might lift up
to our lips and walk
with for awhile,
deeper into the night.

Lately, I've been fishing around
in the briny pages of Oliver,
Nye, Stafford, Berry, and Bly,
if only to catch a whiff
of the wild thing they
were following

and I wonder,
how do they do
what they do?

Asking us to get down on our hands and knees
so that we might see the world from the dome-shaped eyes
of the lowly ant or the California poppy, unfolding
her papery arms to greet the great-hearted sun.

How kindly they demand
that we slow our frantic pace

to admire such ordinary things,

billowing eloquence
at no cost, mind you,
to the procession of
our dignified days.

I may never again
fold the laundry
or finish this
simple line

if I were to live
or love the world
in that kind of way.

RECIPROCITY

Go outside. Kneel
in the grass or
glistening snow.

Press your lips
close to her soft
or prickly skin.

Speak your love
aloud into her
opened ears;

to think these
things alone
is not enough.

Feed her
the way she
feeds you.

Now go.

FACE CONTORTIONS

What is beneath the mask? We all wonder,
but never dare to ask. The perfectly stenciled
eyelids and lips, the over-stretched cheekbones
and once affectable forehead. Now, that sweet distinction

between your rapture and rage
has been firmly betrayed.
You, who've been spoon-fed
images of half-alive women, tricked
into sitting pretty and untethered
in that narrow-waisted corner—
hands idle, soul encaged,
mouth stitched shut.

You, who've been fooled
into believing that youth
is everything;

you, who can blend into
the background of any time
or place, except for the one

that matters.
No wrinkle lines
beside your long-lived eyes;
no wisdom—I mean gray
in your wanting hair.

What are you trying to hide?
Who do you despise?
You, dispirited woman
refusing to age.

Like you I don't want
to hear these things;
I scarcely want to write them.

I don't want to know that we've
been raised by a culture
of commodification,
one that profits mightily
from our implants and insecurities.

I am not here to wave a righteous finger—
I too was once lured into the trap
of self-flagellation. I swam
round and round for years,
nearly drowning in those
shallow waters.

And some days,
if I am not careful,
if I don't read poetry aloud
into the carnivorous air
or gather with other brave souls,
singing a different song into the world,
there is always the danger of being
dragged under all over again.

But we were built for so much more
than this vapid life. More artistry,
bewilderment, humanity, and grace.
We were created to hear the ancient cry
at midnight; to watch the moon walk
her wild way across the blackened sky.

Our hands were designed to weave,
spin, and stir magic into the cauldron
of these well-adorned days. Our lips,
shaped precisely for tasting honey
and the plush silhouette
of mythic prayer.

Our bodies
were meant
to be a vessel,

both filled and emptied
simultaneously

by that which claims
our uncivilized hearts;
by the sunshine, the wind
whipping through the trees,

and the swaying hips of the women who danced,
gathered, cooked, served, painted, and petitioned
every one of our hallowed breaths into being.

THE TRUTH OF NATURE
*In response to The Monet Exhibit at The Denver Art Museum
January 2020*

You have me, oh great brushstrokes
of beauty; spell-casters, dark nights
stretched over long, glistening waters.
You, living things hung on the wall,
watching us watching you.
Oh, how I long to kneel
here on the firm gallery floor

pressing my knees,
then fingertips,
then forehead
onto the gray parting line
drawn out between us,
meant to prevent
hungry ghosts
from stepping in
too close.

How many faces have you seen
longing, swooning, hurting?
Don't let me be just another
that you cast aside. Draw me
deeper into remembering
into this penetrating truth,

reaching out like long arms
through the heart of the world.

Oh brilliant artist, must you insist
on perfecting everything?

How many years of devotion
must lay over one another
to exonerate the unseen?

You remind us of our humanity—
small and forever falling in love
with the peeled back petals
of pink or yellow tulips

and that arc of light,
slanting across the shoulders
of a slowly changing sky.

THE LOVE I KNOW

More times than I can count (or would like to admit),
I have been asked to write and recite love poems
at friends' summertime weddings. "No," is what
I'd like to immediately say. "I don't know how

to make my pen stir towards sap and cliché.
I write about wind, hawks, and the divination
of night; about what it's like to walk the steady body
of a Mountain God where I live; about a heart
beating with so much vigor and purpose that it blasts
right through the cage of your quivering chest—

to throw itself across the forest floor,
bury its red face into a thick blanket
of pine needles, and breathe in
their pungent scent."

This is the kind of love I know and what
my pen sometimes sways for. But of course,
I say yes to the innocent request and proceed

to slide some wooded lavishness
beneath the lines I've been
entrusted to deliver—

into that bright space
beside the whispers,
wilting flowers, and
choked-back tears.

Part 8: Monarch butterflies in North America make southward migrations to overwinter, but no one butterfly can complete the round trip; it takes several generations.

PROVENANCE

If you were to replay
the last third of your life
over and over again
in your mind,

who or what
would you find?

The soft, brown bear searching for food;
your face perpetually fixed for another
strained, but never unpleasant hello.

All those sentences strung together—like broken beads
bumping up against one another on a delicate wire

wrapped around your throat—
promising not to choke.

The twelve months
with their strange texture
on your slack tongue;
the alphabet, forever
slanting toward subservience.

And all those words that
you can never quite remember,
but which you reach for anyway;
hands spread in the direction
of a disquieting provenance.

How with each passing year your legs grow heavier,
less willing to walk the woodland of your youth. Yet,

that steady presence still stands at your side,
never with the unreasonable expectation
that you should attempt the descent alone.

ELUSIVITY

The circles around your eyes
where tears have declared their
imposition—this is our place to begin.

These lines speak what sadness
you cannot; they croon into the cavern
of your strong-held suffering. In the same way
your lips bite back the words that were given
to you at birth—the ones that kept you

from vanishing
into every other
starless night.

But now I hold in my hands
what was once yours, small
and untouchably bare. What you
tried to keep hidden, you let slip
through your slender fingers,
and somehow I have caught
in that great, unwillful falling.
Now, I cradle what is ours

close to my chest,
like the numinous child
you were never permitted to be.

DIMINISHED

People always want to know
precisely how long it takes me
to weave a basket or belt.
They inquire with inquisitive
eyes, as if disbelieving a thing
could still be done

by the human hand.
They want to know
if I've kept time

with the many hours
my aching back
has hunched forward,

working cramped fingers
into the braided yarn of a blanket
or the tangled mess of thread
that I plead with—bead by bead,
into an article of adornment
for our mortal, yet still
meritable ears.

How many hours do I spend
bowed in the pursuit of beauty?
They probe as if the answer
might be extracted
in some effortless fashion,
bearing no resemblance,
mind you, to the craft itself.

But, no one ever inquires after
how long it takes to write a poem

(a day, a week, an entire life?).
Perhaps they're too afraid

my answer will be too long—

a winding trail
through the thick
and foggy forest,

always fumbling
around in the dark
for the next movement
or mystifying line.

"How long does it take you
to craft a beautiful life?"

I want to ask,
but seldom
know how
or why.

REVELATION

Could it be
that we co-conspire
with our destiny?

That there is participation involved—
a congregation of courtship,
and certainly choice

to stay or flee
or fall

into the quaking psalm
beneath it all.

Could it be
that our destiny
is composed,
line by line,
through the act
of our living?

Like a newly hatched poem
or pure slab of marble,
patiently waiting

for the steady hand, the chisel,
the full-bodied prayer. Images slowly
emerging, then retreating; a pause,
a repetition, the never-before-seen.

The break.
Yes, always
the blessed break
of line and heart and rock,

where a single movement

turns you in a different direction—

obliging your courageous stance to inhabit
a place more discerning than before

and any solitary answer
nodding to a hundred more
unanswerable questions.

The ballad you've been dreaming
all of your life is rolling out now

and now

and now.

RENDERING

There is well-founded honor
in the breadth of your labor,

like wheat waving in the
wind, sending blessings
through the lips
of their many gold
fingertips.

May there be ample space
in these trustworthy days

to sink your teeth and tenuous heart
into the firmament of what matters most.

May you taste the wheat.

Let it pop and crackle
against your contented tongue.
Let your people feed the new life
swelling there at the cave of your throat—

and then bend that life
(like the wheat stalks
swaying with the wind)
toward all that you love.

IN THE VERY END

What will you wrack your mind
with in the very end? Surely, it can't be
the wine and water stains left like scar tissue
on the expensive dining room table, nor

despite your best attempts, the way your hair
scarcely wanted to behave. I'm not even convinced
it will be the well-wrought routine you pledged
so much of your time to or the collection of fine

tea pots you stored away in the cabinet, but never
thought to use. Certainly, not every single grievance
for every single person who dared to wrong you.

No, but maybe the time you made a blueberry cheesecake
and brought it to that party to serve in your mother's good
name. You stood in the corner and watched as they savored

their delicate pieces in silence, only a moan
every now and again to mark their rapture.

How tears came to your eyes
when they sucked their forks clean
and lifted their plates for more.

THE COMPANY WE KEEP

Tiny, fast beating heart.
Gray and green feathers.
Orange head. Eyes wide
blinking back the pain.

I come outside to sit beside you
after the headlong crash into our
bedroom window. I apologize for
the reflective glass, holding up
the sky. I sing you a song

while all your little bird friends
circle round in the trees

singing, too. "Don't die!,"
we yowl. "You are too dear."

I inch closer to keep you
in good company, singing
all the while. An eternity passes
as you turn your head left,
then right, contemplating

if you should choose death
or life. "Life! Life!," we all cry.

Until eventually
you say, "Okay,"

then spread your wings
and fly off into the day.

ACKNOWLEDGEMENTS

To the women who gather with me around this burning flame; who with great heart, eloquence, and bold imagination, commit to Feeding the Fire again and again. Mary and Erica, thank you for saying yes to walking, writing, and swooning at my side; for holding me accountable to the pen, the stage, and the vows that would kill each of us to break.

A deep bow to the many other courageous writers and poets, both past and present, who have profoundly influenced this body of work. A full list of names is far too extensive to include here, but know that your stories and faces are with me each time I approach the page. Bless your brilliance, bravery, and lasting contributions to this world.

To *The Barnhart Concise Dictionary of Etymology*, for your constant companionship. While your name is misleading (as you are anything but concise) your wisdom and weight have kept me honest and in awe. I tip my hat to you, Mr. Robert K. Barnhart, for your immense devotion to the written word.

A gracious thank you to *Orion Magazine* for celebrating the melodic narration of "Origin Stories" and *Wild Fibers* for honoring the craft of "Diminished". It's a true privilege to have these poems gathered into your community of artisans and visionaries.

Lisa, thank you once again for anointing these pages with an image to befit their wildness. You see what I am only able to hear—it's magic in the truest sense of the word. May this collection feed your soul-drenched artistry in return.

Billy, I'm laying down praise and humble appreciation at your dancing feet. Thank you for trusting my poetry with your exquisite music; for accompanying me to the stage and recording studio, where many of these stories were initially heard. Your finely-tuned ear and guitar are great gifts for our world.

To the many others who I've had the good fortune of performing several of these pieces alongside—Oliver, Chad, Brittany, Ellen, Lisa, Mary, Erica, to Terry for providing the grand space, and all of the ones who came to bear witness, bless you. Your eager hearts have irrevocably shaped the landscape of my days.

Pele, I am in awe of your courage and graceful way with words. Thank goodness you found poetry and that it found you. Thank you for saying yes.

For those of you who laid your keen eyes on these poems as they were being sculpted and rearranged—Yasmin, Sarah, Wendy, Trevor, and many others—you have been such an important part of their maturing. Thank you for breathing life into my sometimes withered sails.

Lauren, bless your ecologically sound soul. Your willingness to wade through this babbling stream one last time, is a kindness I will never forget. May you always know you have an ally in wordsmithing and beyond.

To People of the Heart, for your listening bodies and trustworthy faces; for receiving the opening and ending lines so sweetly. You too have nurtured this one into being.

To my amazing neighbors for trading stories, plants, books, and libations. You have all been in the foreground of this writing. Your care, kinship, and cookery have fed the continuation of my work. May the raspberries in your gardens nourish you well for many years to come.

Dad, I adore your big heart; thank you for passing along some of that goodness to me. This legacy of loving the world so deeply is what allows me to write.

Trevor, I will spend the rest of our days finding ways to embody my gratitude for all the blessings you bestow upon our life. You create a true place in our home and hearth for these poems to be born into. You are the protector and provider of such mysteries. I love you always.

ABOUT THE AUTHOR

April Tierney lives on a gorgeous hillside near Lyons, Colorado with her beloved husband Trevor, mischievous dog Brooklyn, and wide web of kin. She is the author of *Singing to the Bones*, and coauthor of *The Wonder Series* and *Exposure*. She is also the cofounder of Fire Feeders, a women's writing collective and collaborative press along the foothills of the Rocky Mountains. April is a devout baker, gardener, craftswoman, and lover of the world.

Printed in Great Britain
by Amazon